PHR/SPHR Study Guide

Best PHR Test Prep to Help You Prepare for the PHR Exam! Get PHR Certification!

By

Matt Webber

Table of Contents

Introduction

Becoming a human resource manager can be a very fulfilling job, but there are certain requirements by different companies for the certification that are needed. The PHR Certification Exam is required in order to get an SPHR or PHR certificate. Not every human resource position requires this certification, though it can certainly help with different areas of expertise as well as making one applicant more experienced versus others.

The test is 225 multiple-choice questions, and they have to be answered within four hours. The questions are randomly generated, and each test is unique. In order to pass the test, a score of 500 out of 700 is required. The best way to ensure that the test is passed on exam day is to make sure you study, and you practice with other similar tests. There is no luck or chance involved, and the only way to be sure the information is known and understood is to apply it to concepts seen in various practice tests.

This book is best paired with the practice test

associated, but the independent questions are important as well. In addition to passing the exam to receive certification, one must also have one of the following:

- 4 years professional HR position + a high school diploma

- 2 years professional HR position + bachelor's degree

- 1-year professional HR position + Master's degree or higher.

This study guide will help give an idea of the information that will be on the test, though it is not quite as long. In the other book that goes along with this one, in addition to practice questions, there will also be answers provided with an explanation in order to get a good understanding of what makes the answers correct.

The way this study guide is laid out is in the eight different sections of human resource management that the test will cover. Some parts are longer than others, but they each contain valuable information in order to pass the test.

The study guide will give bits of information as a way of reiteration, but it does not provide all information that might appear on the test. Instead, it aims to provide a cohesive layout of what to expect, giving users a great guide for when it comes time to collate tools and materials needed in order to pass the test.

The first part of each chapter will go over the various information that will be needed in order to pass the exam. The first part of the chapter can act as a checklist for all of the information known. If you go through each of the things that are listed and ensure that those areas of study have been carefully looked over, you can be sure that you will pass the exam with flying colors.

The second half of each chapter will go over more specific information that is taken directly from previous test questions. Though there isn't likely going to be an exam that is exactly the same as one that has been given before, knowing which parts of certain areas of expertise that are included on the exam can help ensure that the tester is well prepared before going in for the process. The information will be very similar to what is in the practice guide, so it's important that this is all understood as best as possible.

The information is not to be memorized, but rather, learned and comprehended. Memorization will not help pass the test. The better someone can understand the actual concepts and laws of human resource management, the better they will be able to make sure they get high marks, as well as succeed in their position. Passing the exam is important but earning a certification and actually using it to help a company are much more important than what a score will read.

Still, it's crucial that the test is passed in the first place and following through with this study guide will help testers understand what they need to know before going in for the exam. Some parts might come naturally to certain testers while other sections require more attention. Everyone is different, so make sure to focus on what you need to know in order to get a good score. What might seem challenging to others could be simple information for you, but that doesn't mean that it should be ignored.

After going through this study guide, take the practice test if you have not already. If you have, it's encouraged that you go through it again to revise of important information that might present itself to you once again on test day.

When it comes time to show up for the test, make sure that you are well rested. Some people feel like they should stay up late to keep studying - worrying or having trouble sleeping over what score they might get. Prepare as much as you can for the test but cut yourself off the night before. there's a good chance that you'll do more harm than good if you try to stuff your brain with extra information. You might find yourself stressing over the mere fact that you cannot remember certain things. Don't cause yourself unnecessary panic. Instead, have a relaxing night focused on clearing your head and getting a good night's sleep so that you can show up fresh and alert for the test the next day.

Be prepared with your own pencil as well as a spare in case the first one breaks. You shouldn't need a calculator, but double check with your testing center just to be sure that they'll be providing one for you. Sometimes, you might be recorded, or at the very least, monitored while you take the test. Don't let this act as a distraction and instead focus on reading the questions thoroughly and picking the correct responses. The biggest reason why someone might fail the test is that they weren't prepared, or they got too hung up on specifics, not letting their knowledge do the work. Just remember that you can do this!

Good luck!

Chapter 1 – Business Management and Strategy

The business management and strategy section of this book are very important. It will lay out all aspects of a tester's ability to analyze internal, external, and business metric sources. There might be strategic questions that test a human resource manager's ability to apply correct knowledge to real-life situations. All areas of strategy and strategic management should be known in order to ensure high marks in this area of the test. Whether it's how a human resource manager spends their day, or what plan they're going to use to increase productivity, there is a lot to be known about the business management of a resource manager.

In order to be prepared, a tester must be able to apply industry best practices to general business environments. There will be questions on the test related to this kind of information, and not only will the tester have to know practical and fundamental meanings behind some of these practices, but they will also have to apply them to exemplary scenarios.

The tester should be prepared to understand what might make up a business's core values, mission statements, or overall goals. They should be able to analyze ethical and behavior expectations. This analyzation might come through on a personal level by looking at how different employees interact with each other. It might also be done with data analytics, in which the human resource manager can look at statistical information about their employees and determine a strategy for any conflict they are able to identify.

When it comes to business management and strategy, it is important to understand the importance that stakeholders have in a company. They also need to know the relationships that could be established in order to influence certain aspects of decision making that a manager might have to partake in. Knowing terms like cross-functional stakeholders and behavioral expectations will be important before going into this test.

A human resource manager also has to look at

different data and determine what is useful and what is irrelevant. By doing this, they can better assess what the right conflict resolution to a problem will be. There are some things that can't be understood with data, but a well-trained human resource manager should know how to take all the information that was available to them and apply them to different real-life scenarios. Terms like attrition rates, time to fill, and ROI will all be important to not only memorize but to understand how they might apply in different examples.

Before going into the test, it is important to understand how different cultural impacts might affect business operations. Culture might be based on a certain race, lifestyle, or geographical location. All of these factors need to be considered when evaluating an employee for a specific job analysis. What steps would be taken to do this properly, and what are some of the laws that protect these employees? Information like this will be asked in a fundamental or functional sense, and it should also be understood in an applicable one as well.

How employees communicate with each other and with management is also incredibly important. Are they doing so in a professional manner or are they going about things in a way that could damage the integrity of the company? A skilled human resource manager will look at communication objectively and analyze whether it is productive or destructive.

One of the most important areas of knowledge a human resource manager should have are those ideas based around ethical and professional standards. At the core of what a human resource manager is responsible for is the maintenance of high standards of professionalism and ethics in order to make sure the needs of employees are being met while business strategies are still being properly implemented in a way that will help the company grow and not keep it straggling behind.

What differs from the test now versus ten or so years ago is the use of technology in order to report or record different aspects of human resource management. Before going into the test, familiarize yourself with the quantitative data collecting methods that are popular now among human resource management. Specific brands might not be mentioned, but overall, the tools that someone might use, such as HRIS, are important to understanding to make sure that all questions can be properly answered.

The next section will cover more specific information that has been taken directly from old tests. This information might not be an exact replica of what is to be expected on the new and current exam, however, it will give readers a good idea of the kind of information that the test creators had in mind when writing up questions. This information is the basis for what you should be studying, among other things, in relation to this chapter's title.

Polygraph Tests

In terms of the strategic role of a Human Resources manager, issuing polygraph tests to all employees would not be included. A human resources manager would, however, plan, discover organizational objectives, and determine an employee's resistance to a geographical location.

There are many strategic roles that an HR manager has, but polygraph testing is not one of them. This can be remembered by looking at the core administrative functions of a human resource manager. These include training and development, benefits administration, recruitment, compensation analysis, and general employee administration. Though a polygraph test might occur in one of these stages, it would not be the responsibility of a human resource manager.

Recruitment involves putting the word out there of the job, and initial interviews and background checks. After that, compensation is decided for an individual employee. The benefits are considered at this stage as well.

Once that has all been settled, the HRM will guide an employee through their training and development, and later maintain general employee administration. None of these steps would include giving an employee a polygraph test.

Polygraph tests are rarely done as it is, even in the recruitment phase. If they are given, then a professional will be there to oversee the test is given properly. As a human resource manager, you won't be expected to give a polygraph test.

Forecasting

Forecasting HR demands can be done with productivity ratios, statistical regression analysis, or simulation models. Any of these mathematical methods would aid in forecasting, and an HR manager is also not limited to these three methods. Forecasting is becoming more relevant as more tools emerge for different resource managers. There are always new innovations to collect and analyze data, so it is important to stay informed on the tools out there that could help grow and develop a business.

As HR managers look to the future, they will have to expect that they might have to deal with an older workforce. This is especially true for positions that are long term. As time goes on, the workforce will always become more diverse.

The amount of the workforce that is entry-level or one that lacks skills doesn't have as much of a differentiation through an HR manager's position. Forecasting involves figuring out labor supply projections, staffing requirement projections, and an understanding of external conditions. Forecasting does not include an analysis of a job. The world is changing every single day, but that doesn't mean that everything is always rapidly different.

There are certain HRM trends that are going to stay the same, and that includes workers that lack skills as well as some entry-level workers. Innovations in education, as well as training programs, will alter the way HR managers hire and who they will hire, but what will differ most in the short-term goals of a human resource manager is how they will handle their employees that are older than the original workforce that has been dealt with.

At its core, forecasting is when labor needs are projected and predicted, and the effects that might have on a business are analyzed as well. Once this basic idea has been discovered, it is then up to the HRM to hire staff in order to properly ensure that the labor needs are being met.

The HRM does more than just hire, they also have to ensure that they are taking care of the needs of their current employees while simultaneously looking at how new hirings will affect the current status of work. The HRM also needs to check up on how this labor cost is going to affect other parts of the business, such as sales, office space, and the money needed for different benefits, compensations, and insurances. Forecasting is like looking at the weather forecast, but for HRM, the storm is new hires.

There are many different methods that a human resource manager can use to forecast their individual business. For the most part, it would start with setting a goal of what needs to be predicted. Is the HRM looking at an estimation of market demand, or trying to resolve employee turnover? A productivity ratio would assess the number of employees it takes to get a certain task done.

This would be helpful in determining how many employees are needed to be hired, or what employees could be moved from certain departments. Each of these mathematical methods has a purpose when it comes to forecasting, and it is up to the HRM to make sure that they are looking out for what the best model for prediction would be. The more aware a human resource manager is of all the mathematical methods there are to aid in forecasting, the better they will be able to make predictions for their company.

Strategic Management

Skill variety, task significance, and autonomy are all included in a job characteristics model. Not all are required, but they all qualify as answers to the question. A job characteristics model is comprised of five core job characteristics. These include skill variety, task significance, task identity, autonomy, and feedback. From these five characteristics, there are five work-related outcomes that could be a result of this model as well.

This includes motivation, performance, absenteeism, satisfaction, and turnover. The job characteristics model is a representation of the job characteristics theory. This model has been modified, though the core values are what remains important to HR managers.

An Ishikawa diagram can also be described as a cause and effect diagram. An Ishikawa diagram is one that was created by Kaoru

Ishikawa. All of the types of Ishikawa diagrams show the causes that a specific event might have. A herringbone, Fishikawa, fishbone diagram, or cause-and-effect diagram are all interchangeable terms and are known as Ishikawa diagrams.

Ishikawa forces those that create the diagram to really look at all the causes of a certain problem. By doing this, a human resource manager might find a problem causer that they didn't expect, perhaps in a small department they weren't giving attention to. By looking at more obvious causes and effects, you might miss out on the small things that are really causing serious damage in a certain industry.

Relocation

If someone in a managerial position is analyzing geographic and competitive concerns, they must consider a particular employee's willingness to relocate to certain geographical locations. Restructuring organizationally might be considered after the employee's desires to relocate are learned.

Foot traffic and work-family balance don't

affect what an HR manager might decide. Not every company has the opportunity for relocation, but when it is presented, the HRM needs to ensure there is a proper program that will help this situation. A relocation scenario would involve a relocation package that would present the benefits to an employee that was eligible for relocation.

The better prepared you are as a human resource manager for relocation services, the smoother everything will go over in this sometimes-challenging position. A human resource manager has to be aware of all the possibilities, benefits, and risks that are involved in a potential relocation. Relocation is not meant to be confused with travel opportunities for employees as well.

Organizations

Organization development can be divided into three different categories – technological, interpersonal, and structural. The process to analyze and identify how much human resources is needed is known as human resource planning. This helps make sure an organization can meet its goal while determining how many human resources is needed to meet the objectives.

A human resource manager is responsible for looking over all other staff and making sure their needs are taken care of, they're being compensated, and all rules are being followed in order to make sure that things continue to run smoothly.

A human resource manager is also responsible for themselves! They have to make sure that they are identifying the need for human resources, what the future might require, and how different costs could be cut in their own department. Human resource planning is important in connecting the overall organization to the actual human resources.

Organization development refers to what it sounds like – how to develop organizational practices within a business. It starts with a technological aspect. What can be computerized, digitized, and added online to a storage system? How can technology overall improve organization and the work efforts of the different employees?

The next stage is interpersonal. What is going on with the employees of a company that can be changed to be better organized? Finally, a structural standpoint should be discovered for human resource managers that want to achieve better organization development. What overall, in the structure of the company, needs to be developed in order for optimal organization to be achieved?

Life Cycle

Of the stages of a life cycle of human resource development, middle age is not a stage. Growth, maturity, and introduction are all considered stages. Most businesses go through four stages that affect how they will operate. The first is growth. Whether this is done overnight or over a decade, all businesses go through a period of growth.

In this stage, a human resource manager would be responsible for overseeing the hiring, recruitment, and evaluation of different employees. As a company goes through the second stage, maturity, the HRM will help in maintaining employee needs, ensuring that different aspects of compensation are being taken care of. This might also include the promotion of a business. The third stage, one that not all businesses will meet, is rebirth.

This is when the company gets a new face, whether it's from rebranding, relocating, or recruiting new managerial staff. The HRM in this process will be responsible for looking back on the company and evaluating what needs to be done to make sure it runs more efficiently. The final stage is decline, and in this stage, if it happens, the HRM would be responsible for cutting employees and other costs that would help keep the business alive as long as possible. Downsizing is when there is a reduction in the size of an overall workforce organization.

Downsizing can occur for many different reasons. It might be to cut the costs of a struggling company. There might be a way to increase profit instead, looking at positions that don't hold as much value as others.

Downsizing can also happen during moments of rebranding when computers or other services are used in place of different things that previous employees did. Downsizing staff can be risky for those that have to lose their jobs, but also for the employees left.

They might fear that they are next in line to get cut, or they might have trouble taking on new responsibilities that the other employees left behind. It is not the final decision of a human resource manager to downsize, but it is up to them to make sure that this operation goes smoothly, and no one suffers more than they have to.

Strategy

HRIS stands for Human Resource Information System. This might also be known as a human resource management system (HUMAN RESOURCE MANAGERS). This is in reference to the software and technology used by human resource managers. There is not one specific program necessary for all human resource managers to use, though there are certain favorites.

It's important to know the acronym in order to determine if a technological or interpersonal issue is being discussed in terms of strategic human resource management. Having electronic HR management documentations allows for certain managers to better look over past and future proceedings to ensure that no steps are being missed, and all information is presented.

As more human resource innovation emerges, so does the need to stay technologically advanced. The more aware one human resource department can be with their technologic knowledge, the better equipped they will be to analyze and process relevant data to ensure they are going about things in efficient ways.

Sometimes, this might include collecting data on employee productivity and using numbers in comparable situations. This might not have been seen as much in previous tests, and it can only be assumed that technological innovation as a resource to analyze positions will become more relevant in the following years.

Succession Plans can be described as an anticipation of the staffing requirements a managerial position holds with the development of high-quality employees in order to meet these needs stated. HR Succession Planning looks at employees that can fill the positions of those in a managerial position when they can no longer fulfill their duties.

This might mean setting others up to take over when someone quits or retires. By properly succession planning, human resource managers can make transitions smooth when those who might have held a certain position for decades finally leave. New management can be very tricky for many businesses to recover from, but it is something that can be done without much destruction if there is a proper succession plan in place.

The dislikes of an employee are not part of the development of a business strategy. When developing a business strategy, it is important to look at both the external factors that might threaten a business, as well as the internal systems that could provide strengths and weaknesses to a company.

An external scan might include things like environmental factors, demographics, competitors, and basic geographical locations. Internal scanning requires businesses to look inward, seeing what weaknesses might hold them back. This could be things such as not having enough of a budget, lack of experience, or unavailability of certain resources. These two scans are very important in order to produce a quality business strategy.

Hofstede's IBM Employee Study

The five dimensions taken from Hofstede's IBM employee study are: uncertainty avoidance, long-term orientation, power distance, individualism, masculine/feminine.

In Hofstede's cultural dimensions, an uncertainty avoidance is in reference to how a society is able to tolerate all of the uncertainty that comes along with day to day operations. You can never predict if there's going to be a hurricane that wipes out a plant, or a manager that needs to take sick leave for a month at a time.

We might be able to make certain predictions based on guesses, but there will always be a level of uncertainty. Uncertainty avoidance is in reference to how the members of a culture program might feel about their comfortability level in various situations that don't seem to have any structure.

Hofstede's IBM employee study aimed to see how different cultures were affected by systematic differences. His analysis produced four dimensions on which national cultures differentiated. The first was uncertainty avoidance. This is how comfortable certain people are with change or the uncertainty level of different aspects of life. The second is long-term orientation, or how someone might plan for the future.

The third is power distance, which is how others influence those around them, and what level they're comfortable doing so. How willing are people to accept inequality? The fourth is individualism, which is all about personal needs and whether or not someone's personal goals are being met versus the overall goals of the organization. The final dimension is masculine/feminine, which looks at how masculine and feminine rules determine different cultural aspects.

Types of Organizations

An organization that would be considered a "prospector" would include the HR practice of external staffing. External staffing is when there is a recruitment of those outside a company to fill positions needed, rather than looking within a company.

This is different than just hiring for an open position. Sometimes, it means looking elsewhere for a manager rather than at a staff that might have years of experience. A company that is a prospective one is one that is looking for innovations and new ways to boost their product or service. They might consider external staffing as a way to bring fresh life into a company that desperately needs a change.

Identifying the type of organization that makes up a company is important for human resource managers so they can properly assess and analyze all the tools needed to help make sure that the company is continually growing and positively expanding.

Chapter 2 – Workforce Planning and Employment

Workforce planning and employment refer to the way that a human resource manager goes about planning their strategies that are going to be used to reach their goals and finding the right employees to help do this. This section covers any recruitment, promotion, hiring, organizing, and orientation, as well as an exit strategy that might be integrated into a business for when an employee decides to go their separate ways.

A human resource manager knows that success comes from the team that helps drive a business and not always just who is on top. A human resource manager will do a fair job in the hiring process, abiding by all the rules put in place to protect the people from any unfair discrimination when it comes time to find the right position.

This section will also look at how much human

resources a business might need. Not only do human resource managers have to plan for the company, but they also have to look out for themselves and their own schedules.

A human resource manager will know what to look for when it comes time to fill staff. The right people will have the right set of skills, and anything they lack can be made up for in the training process that a human resource manager might help to create.

This section on the test will go over the responsibilities that a human resource manager might have. Though responsibilities might change slightly from one position to the next, there are some key aspects of the human resource position that will hold true no matter where someone might be working. They are responsible for workforce planning and the employee activities that occur, as well as making sure all of this is legal and compliant with any federal laws in place.

This section of the test might force the tester to use their knowledge of these federal laws and apply them to real-life scenarios. Some laws can be up for interpretation, and in a real-world scenario, there might be leniency one way or another. What's most important is looking at the core values and ideas that make up a law, ensuring that the basic understanding is known so application can be done on the test.

Employment law is a part that can trip up a lot of people on the test, so if this is an area of struggle, it's important to put emphasis on this during the study. There are many different sections of laws that change and amend throughout time, so staying up to date with all of these is crucial for anyone that wants to pass the test.

Uniform guidelines, employment law, the civil rights act, and other standards that are legally mandated are all things that should be known. Even for those that don't ever expect to work in a large company, or someone that has a job in a location that doesn't require uniforms, it's important to be aware of all these different types of rules and regulations in order to have a decent understanding when it comes time to take the test.

Different types of validity should be known, such as predictive validity, construct validity, content validity, and criterion-related validity.

These forms might get mixed up on the test, so it's crucial to not get caught up too much with various small differences in words.

Governing EEO laws might make up a large section of the test. It's different every year but focusing on this particular section has been consistent among many different test taker's tales. Title VII is a big one to study, but we will also touch on it a little more in depth in this book.

Quid Pro Quo

A quid pro quo can also mean "this for that." Sympathy, whistleblowing, and reasonable person are all terms that have different meanings. A quid pro quo is a favor that is given but with the expectation that the same favor will be returned or repaid in another way. "This for that," is another way to explain this, as you might say, "if you give me this, I'll give you that."

In terms of human resource management, this is something that has to be familiar in order to ensure it is not taking place in the workplace. Most often, a quid pro quo is seen when a manager offers something to an employee in return for a sexual, or otherwise illegal, favor. This form of harassment can be very dangerous, as the employee might feel fearful to tell the HRM of the harassment out of fear of losing their job. Unfortunately, a quid pro quo is the most common form of harassment in different work environments.

There are many other forms of harassment, threat, and blackmailing that might be done in a work environment. Those taking this test should be sure that they are aware of all the steps involved in a harassment case. It starts with identifying the problem and figuring out if it qualifies as a reportable case. After that there needs to be a mediation between those that were involved, with a conflict resolution to follow. There might be different policies in place depending on different organizations, but those taking this exam should still make sure they have a general understanding of harassment and what's needed to properly handle this situation.

FLSA

According to the United States Department of Labor's website, "The Fair Labor Standards Act (FLSA) establishes minimum wage, overtime pay, recordkeeping, and child labor standards affecting full-time and part-time workers in the private sector and in Federal, State, and local governments."

This is just one of the many parts of the Act, and though not all sections need to be memorized, they do need to be known. It is better to memorize them in order to catch sneaky questions that might switch around wording, but really, a basic understanding of when the law or amendment came about, what inspired its creation, and how it currently affects workers should help the exam taker to properly answer any question pertaining to a legal issue.

This would protect any overtime pay that an employee deserves and the record keeping involved in their employment history. It would also include administrative concerns, as well as an employee's status, in reference to if they are part-time, temporary, or on a working visa. The FLSA does not include any retirement plans, as that would be more between the relationship with the employee and their employer, or with a different independent retirement plan they are working with.

Most employees are protected by the FLSA, meaning they are nonexempt. Nonexempt positions are entitled to overtime pay. If more than 40 hours of work are given in a pay week, that employee is entitled to pay that is at least time and a half, though some companies might have different overtime incentives.

Either way, the FLSA mandates that nonexempt employees receive what they deserve when overtime work is given. Exempt employees are those that earn a salary of $23,660 per year, or more. These workers are not protected under the FLSA, though many companies will still offer overtime pay if a certain number of hours are worked, as an employee incentive.

If someone partially works their weekly hours as well as a combination of cashing in on vacation hours for their weekly salary, they wouldn't be entitled to overtime, even if they got paid for more than forty hours in a week.

For example, someone that works 39 hours in a week and uses 2 vacation hours would not be entitled to that extra hour of overtime pay, since the hours weren't technically worked. Getting paid time and a half doesn't qualify as overtime either.

Overtime is only given when someone actually works more than forty hours in a week, and they are nonexempt. There might be situational examples on the test that could slip up some takers, so it's important to be aware of how to apply these rules and laws to real-life situations.

Many employees are given a salary, which is usually an amount slightly higher than what the average total amount of a 40-hour minimum wage paycheck would be. A salary is usually referred to in annual terms, meaning if a person gets paid $1,000 a week, they have a salary of $52,000 a year.

This form of payment is mostly given to professional and white-collar workers. Not everyone in a company gets paid the same, so some employees might make a salary while others receive an hourly fee. Getting paid a salary will usually be part of a compensation package that also includes other benefits, such as paid vacation, healthcare, and other forms of insurance.

The FLSA regulates overtime pay, recordkeeping, administrative concerns, and employee status. FLSA is not responsible for the retirement plans of employees, work-related injuries that might have caused an employee to take out worker's compensation, or the familial affairs of their employees.

The Fair Labor Standards Act is one of the most important acts for Human resource managers to be aware of in order to ensure their employees most basic rights are being met within a corporation. This includes adhering to a federal minimum wage that must be met, with very few exceptions in place.

This also makes sure recordkeeping is being kept and properly recorded in order to ensure that the rights of employees are being protected. The FLSA is also responsible for establishing child labor standards and restricted hours for children of a certain age. Though there are more important factors within this act, these are the most basic to understand and remember.

Nonexempt positions, according to the Fair Labor Standards Act, would be positions that perform clerical, routine, or manual work during a percentage of their time. Overtime pay, children's work hours, and minimum wage regulation are all protected under The Fair Labor Standards Act.

Short-term disability would be how a pregnancy is treated according to The Pregnancy Discrimination Act of 1978. The Pregnancy Discrimination Act of 1978 states:

> "The terms 'because of sex' or 'on the basis of sex' include, but are not limited to, because of or on the basis of pregnancy, childbirth, or related medical conditions; and women affected by pregnancy, childbirth, or related medical conditions shall be treated the same for all employment-related purposes, including receipt of benefits under fringe benefit programs, as other persons not so affected but similar in their ability or inability to work."

This protects employees that are pregnant or

choose to become pregnant from discrimination. In order to go through the proper paperwork, Human resource managers are encouraged to treat a pregnancy such as a short-term disability, meaning that the employee will be back to work after a period of time has been taken off. This will be seen in many sections throughout this quiz.

Learning about the compensation, bonuses, and benefits that new parents and families in general receive is important in order to pass the test. This is a huge part of human resource management, so it is going to appear on the test often as well.

Job Analysis

A job analysis does not include obligations certain tasks carry. A job analysis would include investigating a way to gather information about the content of a job, a systematic method of analyzing human requirements, and the context in which jobs are performed.

In a job analysis, the certain duties required by a position are identified. Looking at what duties, jobs, specifications, and responsibilities of a position are important in order to collect data and analyze what parts of a position are required, and which can be cut down. Is a person getting paid enough, or is there a way that hours should be cut in order to save money?

By figuring out an in-depth job analysis, human resource managers are able to decide who is the best fit for a certain position and who would be better suited elsewhere. A job analysis differs from a job description in that it is more in-depth, and a process performed by a human resource manager, rather than a job description that would simply list the duties and expectations of a certain position.

During a job analysis, a human resource manager might need to determine what the most important position in a company might be. In order to do this, they might use a point factor method. This would first involve selecting a job cluster of the company. From there, the HRM would pick out factors of each of those jobs and determine a degree or scale of what makes these compensable.

Different weights would be given to different aspects, and from there, a score can be added to determine which positions hold the most value. This is always important to do to ensure that fair labor is being given as well as fair compensation. Doing this once doesn't mean that it doesn't need to be done again. It should be something included annually, if not more.

Job Description

A job description is necessary in order to weed out potential candidates that wouldn't be a good fit for a position. At any given time, there are many people on the hunt for a new job. Not every single one of these people is going to be a good fit, or even qualified, for certain positions.

The more detailed a job description, the better a chance for employees that are actually good candidates to get an interview time in. A job description will list the responsibilities of that position, and their purpose and relation to other positions in the company. How often someone is interacting with the public or working in a team will usually be specified in a job description as well.

The qualifications needed, whether it's a degree, certificate, or a number of years of experience will also help make a job description more detailed to ensure that only those that qualify will be able to get an interview slot. A job description might include a salary listed, though this is often something that is going to be discussed after the first interview when abilities are determined.

Predictive Validity

Predictive validity best describes an index number that is given to the relationship between a predictor and the criterion variable. As a human resource manager, it is important to understand all the ways that different employee data analytics can be predicted and analyzed. All different forms of validity should be studied and understood so they could be properly applied in different situational examples.

Depending on a human resource manager's objective, there is likely going to be a different method of achieving the information that is desired. Sometimes, this information isn't going to be completely accurate, but in other instances, it might even be spot on. Predictive validity refers to the efficiency in which a test is conducted and the information that is measured. Predictive validity looks at how that tool was used to achieve the desired information, and whether or not it did the job it needed to do. By doing this assessment, it can be better determined how results might be achieved better the next time a human resource manager is collecting data. Looking towards the future of a company is an important role for a human resource manager, and predictive validity can help assess the productivity of an HRM's fortune-telling abilities.

Discrimination

Sex, racial and ethnic, and age discrimination are all considered types of employment discrimination. Hiring only young, thin, attractive women can be a form of disparate treatment. Sexual harassment and intentional treatment might also be exhibited in addition to this, but they aren't necessarily inherent or the same thing as disparate treatment. Disparate treatment and disparate impact are two different terms that need to be differentiated, as there might be a trick question that combines the two on the actual exam.

Disparate treatment is when there is an intentional discrimination in the employment process. It might involve testing certain sexes or minorities in different areas rather than testing all employees equally. Someone that wants to only give background checks to African American applicants would be practicing disparate treatment.

Disparate impact occurs when there is more of an unintentional discriminatory practice in place. A disparate impact is one that might eliminate a certain protected group during the interview process because of a requirement that would likely make them ineligible. For example, imagine an electrician who's reaching the age of retirement, but he's not ready to end his career.

The electrician's managers fire him and justify doing so because he received several complaints. They are allowed to fire him, however, if there are several other employees that are younger than him with the same amount of complaints, and the company doesn't fire them, they are exhibiting a disparate impact.

Discrimination doesn't stop at the hiring process. Discrimination comes in many different forms, is sometimes obvious and other times challenging to identify. An experienced HRM will know how to spot discrimination and what makes up a discriminatory act. If any discrimination is even sensed, it is always worth investigating.

Those that are discriminated against belong to a protected class, which includes, women, minorities, and those part of the LGBTQA community. Discrimination could be as subtle as not giving off a requested vacation day to someone in a protected group, or it could be as large as firing someone because they are homosexual.

No matter the degree of discrimination that an employee faces, action must be taken by a human resource manager to protect the worker's rights and the integrity of the company.

Interview

A targeted selection interview uses questions to investigate what an employer might have done in other positions that are related to the job being interviewed for. A group, phone, and situational interview all use different methods of gaining information about potential candidates.

A target selection interview allows the employer to determine the specific points of a job and how well a person might be able to fulfill those duties. In a target selection interview, the previous jobs and duties that someone went through in their past positions will provide examples of how they might perform in the next position.

Not only does this allow an employer to better determine if the person they are interviewing is right for the position, but the potential candidate also has the opportunity to meet management and see if the job is really something that they are interested in after all.

These are common types of interviews, though there are many others that have their own benefits as well. It's important to go into the test knowing about all the different types of interviews in order to ensure that preparation is met for the test.

A behavioral interview is one that takes place in the hiring process when an employee gets asked about their past behavior. A behavioral interview is probably one of the most common types of interviews that many employers use to get to know different candidates.

In a behavioral job interview, candidates will be asked about how they might have reacted in previous situations that aren't even related to the workforce. This is to gauge what they might be like in different situations.

If someone is making a judgment, for instance, in a job interview a rating might be done, and that judge lets their personal interest affect their professional score, this would be known as a rater's bias.

As a human resource manager, it is crucial that personal ideas don't interfere with a rating that might be given to an employee on a professional level. For instance, if an employee has a certain tattoo of a band that the HRM doesn't like, this should not affect the way they perceive that employee.

If tattoos are permitted, nothing about the personal taste of that employee should affect how a human resource manager treats them, so, during an employee review, small personal distaste among the two should be kept out of the equation. If not, a rater's bias might occur, giving the employee an unfair disadvantage.

Performance Appraisal

Performance appraisal is another way of saying "employee evaluation." Job design, HR strategic management, and 360-degree feedback all refer to different things but don't mean the same thing as an employee evaluation.

Performance appraisal is used to measure an employee's adherence to the performance standards put in place. A performance appraisal gives an employer the chance to address the issue of an employee failing to adhere to the performance standards.

This appraisal might happen yearly, monthly, or not at all, depending on the company. An appraisal has no legal definitions, and what might be involved is different among various institutions. It might be done with a direct supervisor, or it could occur with an entire group of the heads of the department.

It's important for a human resource manager to be aware of the various things that might be discussed within a performance appraisal, so they can ensure they're being fairly and properly conducted.

In a performance appraisal, an employee's contribution to the company, as well as overall job performance, will be evaluated. Because this is similar to an employee evaluation, the two terms can be interchangeable.

Sometimes, these reviews might happen annually, or they could happen every month. Sometimes, reviews will be face to face, but they also might be completed through documents. The point of doing a performance evaluation is to ensure there aren't any problems that need addressing between management and an employee.

Areas of strength and weakness can be discussed in a performance review, allowing for both the company and the employee to continually grow. There are three key functions that must be addressed in a performance appraisal. The first one being feedback and needs to be provided to both the employee and the employer.

What does each think of the others' performance? The second key function is to allow for the modification of working habits or a work environment. The third function is one that provides data to the manager and the HRM to use for future assessment. It gives a basis for comparison so that each job assessment becomes more functional.

Types of Employment

Job sharing is an example of an alternative work schedule. Self-employment, self-directed task force, and remote are all terms that have different meanings than "alternative work schedule."

An alternative work schedule is one that includes a full work week completed in a condensed amount of time. Instead of working a full 40-hour workweek within five days, it might be completed in three. Any form of a compressed work schedule would be considered alternative.

Job sharing is in reference to more than one employee that shares the duties of a full-time position. For example, two people might work 20-hours within a three-day period, completing the tasks that someone might have needed 5 days for if it were one full-time employee.

Working remotely could be considered an alternative work schedule, but only if that employee chooses to do their full-time work within a short period of time.

An independent contractor is someone that is contracted by an employer for a certain duty, task, operation, or goal. They are hired on as a non-employee and are only brought in to take on that certain task. Sometimes, an independent contractor might work for a company more than once if the employer enjoys their work.

For example, someone working at a video

production company might get hired to help light sets, but they wouldn't be given a consistent position and would instead continue to find their own work elsewhere. They would likely bring some of their own lights and would have to make sure all their projects would allow for a new position to be taken on. They might never hear from the employer again for another project, or they might get hired every other month when their work is needed.

A closed shop refers to a union that requires hired employees to join the union upon hiring. It does not refer to an old union, a closed store, or a union that does not allow any new members.

In a closed shop, there will be a predetermined agreement between the union and employers in which they will only hire those that are going to become union members. In a closed shop, employees must also remain a member of that union, meaning from beginning to end, they are in agreement with their union.

By doing this, it keeps the union stronger and allows for the union to also have more of a say in who is a good candidate to hire. This is not always the case with how unions work, so it is important to know all of the different kinds of unions and what agreements come along with each different type of union shops.

Chapter 3 – Total Rewards

Total rewards refer to any and all ways that an employee receives what they need in order to compensate them correctly for the work that they have done. The reason we all work is just to get paid, so this area is certainly important for human resource managers to be aware of all areas of compensation, benefits, and payroll. Sometimes, a human resource manager might be directly responsible for payroll, or there might be a team of people implemented to send out paychecks. Either way, it's crucial that a human resource manager is aware and understanding of all aspects of payroll.

Aside from just how someone makes their money, a human resource manager needs to know what different amounts of compensation employees are entitled to when they experience different levels of injury, promotions, or other events that entitle them to a different amount of pay than what they are used to.

Human resource managers should also be aware of how to maintain fair pay and how to look into a case in which someone is not receiving what they are owed. They will have to oversee the different ways in which someone might be compensated while making sure that everything is handled professionally and legally.

Sometimes, a human resource manager might be a part of different negotiations that involve getting paid more or receiving more benefits. They must know the procedures that are put in place in order to protect workers as well as the employers that are doing the check-signing.

All aspects of compensation programs, rather it's implementation, promotion, management, or compliance, is dealt with in a human resource department. Giving compensation is important because it is what the employee usually cares about the most. All federal laws need to be followed during this process as well, so the test taker needs to be aware of different rules and regulations that affect employee's compensation amounts.

It is also up to the human resource manager to promote other forms of cash rewards. There might be a way to pay off tuition within a working environment, or volunteering time could count towards bonuses as well. There might be different kinds of workplace amenities which could include a gym or healthy snacks that would count towards the compensation that an employee receives. It is also the duty of the human resource manager to give out different rewards bonuses, such as extra store credit when a certain sales goal has been met.

A human resource manager needs to know all about the different implementation of an employee's benefit program. This means making oneself aware of the different healthcare plans available, and what sort of vision/dental/or retirement plans that a person is entitled to within their company.

Budgeting is going to be a large part of a human resource manager's job, as well as a subject that will be discussed on the test. The more a human resource manager knows about this subject, the better they will be able to run the company efficiently. Budgeting directly ties into payroll, and there are many laws that also protect payroll that a human resource manager needs to be aware of.

There are some specific accounting practices that a human resource manager might be in charge of as well, in association with different compensation packages. All forms of accounting need to be understood in order to ensure that those taking the test are able to pass this particular area.

Indirect and direct compensation need to be differentiated, and non-cash compensation should be understood at the core as well. Benchmarking compensation and benefits, and the methods in which these two are aligned should be understood as best as possible.

Some of these aspects will be discussed in the following sections, but anything that there isn't time to touch on should be closely studied for anything that a test taker is not aware of.

Compensation

Transportation costs would not be addressed in a compensation program. Legal compliance, equity for employees, and cost-effectiveness might all be factors that would be addressed in a compensation program.

A compensation program would include how

and what an employee is going to be paid. It might include any legal compliances that the company would cover for their employees. There is also a chance that it would consider different equity for employees, as well as the cost-effectiveness of certain other programs that exist within the compensation plan.

A human resource manager would be responsible for overlooking different compensation programs and would have to be sure that they are creating something cost-efficient and fair enough to cover what the employee is entitled to.

Executives receive more variety of compensation programs that are available as compared to the other employees in the firm. Executives do not receive a strict flat rate among the top ten highest paid employees in a company, nor do they receive a paycheck exempt from federal taxes. An executive might get compensation paid quarterly, but this is not necessarily an executive standard.

Executives are paid much differently because there is usually an element of incentive involved for the executive to perform, or encourage their staff to perform, more efficiently to turn a higher profit. Long-term cash incentives are involved in executive corporations, as well as global compensation.

There is no standard for an executive compensation, but it will typically involve many more benefits and luxuries than other employees in the company. The pay packages are much more diverse, and it's important to know what might be involved in order to differentiate from other employee compensation programs.

Long-term incentive pay is best described as a form of direct compensation. Direct compensation refers to any instance that money is directly paid to an employee. Most often, this includes salaries, wages, commission, and bonuses. Indirect payment involves something that isn't liquid paid to an employee. This would include maternity leave, other flexible benefits, and worker's compensation. Long-term incentive pay refers to anytime an executive is paid for achieving certain goals or milestones. These usually include strategic objectives and performance goals that will motivate the executive to increase profit among the company, therefore promising long-term incentive pay. What makes up a long-term incentive pay program is different, but it is still referred to as a form of direct compensation.

Unemployment compensation covers when employees are laid off even though it's not their fault whatsoever. In some cases, a human resource manager might be involved in the process of laying off different employees. This is an unfortunate time, but there is at least compensation to be given to employees that experience this layoff. This is referred to as unemployment compensation.

This is usually calculated by taking gross wages in two different quarters, dividing by 2, and multiplying by .03. Unemployment does not pay as much as normal compensation, and the terms will be different based on an employee's length with a company, ability to find more work, and how much they had to be made within the rest of the year. Sometimes, severance packages are given during layoffs, but these are not to be interchanged with unemployment compensation.

Indirect Compensation

Indirect compensation is a way of stating benefits. The bonuses that come along with a company would be referred to as the indirect benefits that are associated with a certain position. Unpaid leave, social security benefits, and differential pay would all present themselves in cash or check form.

Indirect compensation might be the price taken off a medical bill that was covered by insurance, or a bonus like a company car or phone that the employee can use at their own discretion. Different forms of indirect compensation should be known in order to pass the test better.

The Equal Pay Act

The Equal Pay act will help with compensation associated with discrimination. According to the U.S. Equal Employment Opportunity Commission, the Equal Pay Act of 1963, "prohibits sex-based wage discrimination between men and women in the same establishment who perform jobs that require substantially equal skill, effort and responsibility under similar working conditions." This was enacted in 1963 in order to protect the rights of workers. Though dates can sometimes be hard to memorize, the test often asks for different dates as a way to test memorization skills of the test taker.

The Equal Pay act was put in place in order to make sure that everyone would be paid fairly in an organization no matter their race, sex, age, or any other reason that someone might discriminate against them. However, there are some exceptions that define that certain differences in pay aren't considered wage discrimination. One exception is seniority pay.

This means that certain people that were in a company longer than others are entitled to a higher pay because of their seniority. A merit system is another exemption from a different wage gap, meaning that an employee's job performance will determine how they might get paid. Certain factors within these exemptions might be subjective, which is where the importance of a human resource manager comes in to make sure that the exemption is legitimate.

The Equal Pay Act was put in place in order to make sure that those with the same skills, effort, and responsibilities are protected. An exemption from The Equal Pay act would be overtime.

An equal employment opportunity survey is one that might be required to be filled out by various institutions on a regular basis. For example, a bank that issues U.S. savings bonds might be required to fill one out annually. This survey will help determine the different demographics of a job, including what race, ethnicity, and gender are present in a certain work environment, ensuring there is equality among employees and the various positions.

By implementing this survey in different positions, employees can be sure that they will be protected from discrimination, and the public that might be involved with these positions also can be certain that there will be a diverse workforce that won't discriminate against them either.

Payroll

Payroll involves how a person might get paid. Sometimes, this might be done through different programs, or it might involve straight up handing someone a signed check. No matter what the method is for how an employee might get paid, it's crucial that the human resource manager understands every level of this.

That might include taking out a certain amount of taxes, or it could also be in reference to other exemptions that are removed from a paycheck. There are many different aspects that protect a worker's salary and wage, so the human resource manager needs to know all of these in order to properly assess whether or not someone is being paid correctly.

The Davis-Bacon Act of 1931

The Davis-Bacon Act of 1931 is most relevant to companies that are firms currently engaged with federal construction projects, and only those whose projects exceed the cost of $2,000. This also states that the "prevailing wage," is a rate that must be paid.

The Davis-Bacon Act is important in protecting federal workers, ensuring that they are entitled to minimum wage standards even when not working full-time positions. This Act emerged in 1931 and states, "contractors and subcontractors performing on federally funded or assisted contracts in excess of $2,000 for the construction, alteration, or repair (including painting and decorating) of public buildings or public works."

Person-Based Pay System

A system that doesn't pay employees based on the tasks that are currently performed, but rather based on what employees are capable of doing is known as a person-based pay system.

A person-based pay system might involve an employee getting paid more based on the experience or skill level that they have. This might also include getting paid more based on a certification or degree that someone has. It cannot be based on any sort of discriminatory reasons, such as a person's age or sex.

Benefits

Holiday bonuses would not be considered legally mandated benefits. Social security, worker's compensation, and unemployment compensation would all be considered legally mandated benefits.

Legally-mandated benefits, also known as legally required benefits, is anything that is required to cover the treatment of different aspects of healthcare. These might include social security, Medicare, or the Federal Insurance Contributions Act (FICA). This is what's often taken out of employee's checks in order to go to other services.

Holiday bonuses and other forms of compensation that are "extra" features would not be considered legally mandated benefits. This can be remembered by thinking of the basic needs that need to be taken care of. Lower-income families, the elderly, and those that are disabled still need to receive money, which is where legally mandated benefits would come into effect.

Packages

A benefits package can be great for the employee receiving this form of compensation. Having insurance brings peace of mind as well as many other factors that would improve a worker's mood while working. Aside from benefits to the employee, there is also a good reason that a company would want to offer their employees a fair benefits package. The main reason would be that it would help reduce turnover. Employees that are satisfied with the amount they are receiving and the protection that surrounds their health as well of their families will be more likely to stick around a position, meaning that recruitment and training costs can go down.

While many different aspects of a health insurance plan can benefit an employee, it might not always be accepted by the health care provider. A utilization review is a chance for a health insurance company to look over the different requests of medical treatment that an employee might have given.

Sometimes, a recommended treatment might not be the appropriate one to go through with, so in some cases, a human resource manager might have to work with insurance agents to determine whether or not certain aspects of healthcare are required after all.

Health Care

Utilization review is an audit that consists of the services and costs billed by certain health-care providers.

Self-insurance is an example of a funding feature that might be found in a health plan. Self-insurance is when an employee might decide to not take out any health insurance at all, and rather find a third-party to do so. They might not get any insurance at all, though, with the Affordable Care Act, this isn't supposed to present itself as an option anymore.

Employee Assistance Programs

Employee assistance programs help those that

are experiencing emotional, physical, or other personal problems within a company.

A YMCA membership would not be considered a wellness program. Smoking cessation, child care education, or cancer prevention education could be considered wellness programs depending on company policy.

Those in charge of running a company or certain business might want to include some employee wellness programs to ensure that their staff is healthy and happy. These are programs paid for by the employers and are not things that can be traded for cash or liquified.

For example, an employer might want to hold a cancer prevention meeting in which a professional discusses ways in which employees can prevent themselves from getting cancer. By having educated employees, the employers can be certain that they are doing their best to maintain workers that will live long and remain productive. An onsite fitness center, availability of different types of snacks, or even just having a place where employees can take naps would all be considered a type of employee wellness program.

Employee assistance programs, which might

also be referred to as EAPs, are voluntary and work-based programs that offer assessments, counseling, and referrals, usually those that are anonymous. These programs might begin because someone is experiencing work or personal problems.

These programs are paid for by the employers and allow them to make sure that any issues that are affecting their employees can be properly taken care of to ensure that there is no hold-up in the work process.

Chapter 4 – Training and Development

Not only is employee training important, but the development of how that training is going to occur is crucial as well. All of the ways in which employees can learn different knowledge and train in different areas should be well known by a human resource manager that is going to be taking the test.

Finding talent can sometimes be challenging, but that is why it is so important for a human resource manager taking the test to know how to find the right employees that would align with the goals of the company. Training employees can be challenging and different methods for one company might not always be effective for another. It is up to a skilled human resource manager to be able to decipher which training program would work best for a specific organization. In order to do this, different studies should be looked at as well as other methods of training including diagrams and charts.

There are many different training and development methods that someone could use in a company, but it's important to have a basic idea of all these strategies in order to ensure that they can be easily applied during the taking of the test.

Training and development are both crucial to the roles of a human resource manager, but the two are different from each other. Development refers to the preparation and learning an employee goes through when they have already been working for a business. They might undergo development in order to train for a new position, or just to improve the quality of their work.

Development might include seminars, conventions, or presentations that can increase skill and knowledge. It might be recertification or requiring a higher degree in order to improve the overall knowledge a certain employee has. Training would refer to all of this before, or at the beginning of, the hiring of a new employee.

Training is defined as learning skills that apply to an employee during the current job.

Individual learning experiences, preparation of an employee's future career, and the education required to get a certain degree would not be considered training in terms of an HR position.

Training is the process in which an employee learns a particular new set of skills and tools that will be applicable to their time employed with the company. A human resource manager is responsible for setting up an employee's training, but they might not always be the ones in charge of making sure that an employee is trained.

For some companies, a human resource manager will also look at the learning skills that apply to an employee during the current job and figure out whether or not training programs are efficient. A human resource manager will work with those that train others to make sure that the process is going as smoothly as possible so as to make sure the new employee can start regular work as soon as possible, without compromising the learning of any important skills that will help the company improve and grow.

Training is important for obvious reasons, including the necessity to make sure that workers know what they're doing within a certain company. It is also important for a business in an individual sense, as it allows for the business to receive certain benefits as well.

If there is an overall reduction of errors, that means less money is to be wasted and fewer supplies will be used in order to retrain employees or get the risk management involved as it might take time to resolve an issue. There is also less employee turnover. During training, the employee gets the chance to really see what working that position is like, so if they don't like what it involves, they can leave before they become too committed.

It also gives them the chance to get comfortable, so they find it easier to adjust to the certain requirements that a job might include. These are just a few of the benefits of training that should be known by a human resource manager in order to have a high level of knowledge to pass the test.

In 1959, Donald Kirkpatrick created a model that could be used to effectively evaluate the methods of training that a particular company has. By using this model, HRM managers and trainers can look at their training methods objectively to determine whether or not they are effective.

The first criterium in the model is reaction. This takes into account how people might be feeling about a training program and whether or not it is something they are comfortable with. The second criterium is learning. Are people actually learning something from this method of training? The third is behavior.

Are people behaving differently than they did before the training programs? The fourth is results. This might include data analytics that look at the results of a certain training method in order to see if there are actually results coming from what was learned and practiced.

Job analysis is not one of the three phases of training. The three phases of training include planning, implementation, and evaluation. The first phase involves assessing an organization and the training needed to be done. Different employees require different levels of training.

The second step would be implementation, which is the process of training being done. This might include a weeklong training program or one that takes months at a time. The third step would be evaluation, where it is determined whether this training method is effective or not. There are different processes within each of these steps, but they are all individually important to understand on their own level.

Training has benefits that include a reduction in errors and employee turnover. Turnover, in terms of employment, refers to the act of using a new employee as a replacement for the old. Turnover looks at the number of employees that enter and exit a particular company and the rate at which this happens. Certain positions might have a high turnover, like a fast food restaurant or a retail shop.

Other positions might not have any turnover at all, with the same employees for years at a time. Some positions, like seasonal jobs, might not be affected by turnover as much as others. There are many businesses, however, that might suffer the most from high turnover rates. Recruiting, interviewing, and training all take time and money from a business, so if this has to happen often, profit might not be as high as it could be.

In order to ensure there isn't a problem with the company, a human resource manager should track turnover rates. This can be done with this formula: (Number of terminations) (100) / (average number of employees).

The Learning Process

For some companies, the four phases of learning might differ a bit, but there are certain key elements that can be seen in four different steps. The first involves unconscious competence, which might include a form of preparation. Inciting interest in the company might also be included in this first step.

It might involve a trainer going over what is involved in a day-day operation for a certain business with the new employee. The second stage of learning is coming face to face with these new skills, which is when hands-on training might start. The third would be application and using this new knowledge or set of skills to actually go out there and begin working.

The final stage would be using these skills regularly without any practice. In all of the stages, questioning is the most important in order to ensure that continual knowledge is being taken in by the employee.

A training needs analysis would look at the need for training versus employee training. It would identify if a problem would be fixed by further training, or if that would only make things worse in the end, possibly by spending too much time or money that could be used better elsewhere.

There are different analyses that can be used that might help someone determine what the results of a training needs analysis would be. These might include other analysis such as individual, task, or organizational.

Those that are in training go through different stages of learning. It might start with just shadowing someone, for example, in a serving setting. They would follow a staff member around as they wait on tables, making sure to keep in mind the duties and responsibilities they're witnessing and using this for a basis of what they're going to do when training has ended.

After that, they might start actually waiting tables themselves, but still with the help of a trained staff member. This would be referred to as active practice. They are actually taking the skills that they have learned in training so far and actively applying them to the job duties that lie ahead.

Behavior modeling is not a strategy used in the behavior modification approach. A human resource manager needs to be aware of different behavior modification approaches in order to determine how to possibly resolve a conflict. Whether this arises during training or during a time an employee is working that has been around a long time, there are different behavior modification approaches that need to be taken in order to remedy various situations. Punishment might need to be taken, but only in forms of reprimand that might include moving someone to a different position or cutting hours. Both negative and positive reinforcement could also help ensure that behavior changes one way or the other.

Job rotation is when trainees are transferred to a different job in the hopes of broadening their focus as well as increasing their knowledge. Within certain companies, different tasks can be done by employees that have the same training.

By moving around positions, employees get the opportunity to broaden their perspectives and look at what different opportunities there might be within a company. Sometimes, if production seems to be lacking or sales are low, a human resource manager might look at what employees could switch positions. By doing this, it might open up new opportunities for both the employees and the company.

Someone in a retail store might be moved from ready-to-wear to jewelry, where they end up performing much better and drive sales even higher. This can benefit the company's sales and the satisfaction of the employee.

Job enlargement is a job design practice that broadens the scope of a job. Job enlargement describes a technique in which there is an increase in the number of tasks that come along with a certain job. Some might assume that a job enlargement would be the process of increasing employees or the amount of work that a company is putting out, but it's about the increase in work that is taken on by an individual. A job enlargement doesn't always necessarily mean a wage enlargement.

Sometimes it's necessary for production but other times it might be done to cut down costs or increase overall profit.

Bloom's taxonomy describes the levels of learning in six different steps. The first one is knowledge. This is when previously known information is called upon in order for the advancement of more learning. Comprehension is second, which is when more is understood about what is being learned while applying it to what is already known.

The third is application, in which the first and second step are applied to the new presentation at hand. The fourth level is analysis, in which what is learned and what has yet to be learned is identified. The fifth is synthesis and the sixth is evaluation. It is important for human resource managers to know these six steps in order to ensure that employees are learning in a proper and effective way, whether they're just starting a job or improving on the performance that they already give within a certain position.

KSA

Knowledge, skill, and ability are the words in

the acronym KSA. KSA is used often when discussing job duties, evaluations, descriptions, and anything else that might be included overall in a job analysis. The knowledge is what is needed to be known by an employee, either through previous experience or the training that they're going to partake in. Skill involves the set of skills that might be needed by a particular employee in order to ensure that the job is completed. Ability is all about the performance of the employee, whether it's through the expected requirements or through a description of what abilities they might have to possess.

Missions and Goals

A goal is an end and a strategy are how you get there.

Defining purpose as well as laying out the values of an organization could be included in an employer's mission statement. A mission statement is important for any company to have, whether it's been around for a hundred years or is just developing. The mission statement will allow others that don't know much about the business to understand the purpose and direction that the company wishes to go.

A mission statement has three main parts. It will be sure to show the core values that a company holds. What is most important to a company to maintain? The second part would be the goals that a company has. What do they wish to achieve throughout their lifetime?

The third, and most important, is a statement of the objective of the business. A human resource manager should know a company's mission statement inside and out not only to be able to educate new employees but to ensure that the business is also staying in line with their mission statement throughout the ways that they wish to operate.

Operating a program is a cost directly received by employers. A direct cost is one that can be traced directly to the production of a good or service. An indirect cost is one that is needed to keep the business in operation.

Knowing both of these is important for a human resource manager so they can create budgets and determine different costs of different aspects. It is important to know the difference, so you can price different acts of operational organization needed to make sure that budgets and costs are met.

There are many goals that a human resource manager has, but they are generally individual and organizational. The HRM is responsible for ensuring that an organization reaches its goals, while also making sure that the individual needs of the employees are met as well. The HRM is responsible for making sure that organizational human resources are being fulfilled, while also ensuring that there is an attention to individual employee needs and issues as well. A human resource manager isn't responsible for supervisory goals and instead needs to make sure that they are taking care of individual and organizational goals first and foremost.

Every company needs to make sure that they are setting different goals, both at a corporate and an individual level. These goals might not always be met, but they are important to determine what needs to happen within an organization to meet these particular goals.

This might include doubling profits from the

year before, or sometimes even just trying to hire a more diverse set of employees. Before anything else can happen, a goal must be set. Once there is a goal in mind, a strategy needs to be created in order to achieve that goal. A strategy cannot exist without a goal in mind or at least an idea of what one might want to achieve with their specified strategy.

Hawthorne Studies

Hawthorne effect is known as the impact that physical and environmental influence has on employee performance, and in some cases, special notice from a managerial position could help increase motivation in an employee.

The Hawthorne studies is a set of ideas and practices that were studied in Cicero, Illinois at the Hawthorne Works. This study proved that some employees might alter their work if they are aware that they are being watched. The original idea went on to inspire other work-related discoveries, including how a physical and environmental space might affect the employee that's working within that space.

The point of these studies was to focus on the

worker's needs, and they did just that, igniting more studies to determine the best way to keep employees happy and efficient. A human resource manager should be aware of the results of the Hawthorne studies as well as other instances of worker's behavior being observed. The more that is known about the scientific reason a worker might act the way they do, the better a human resource manager can think of a solution to help resolve any issues that might arise, whether they're personal or professional.

The Hawthorne study mainly focuses on analyzing and assessing how physical and environmental factors might affect performance. The Hawthorne study puts emphasis on the socio-psychological aspects that might affect human behavior.

This study was conducted within a workplace and helps other employees with information about how their workers might react or handle certain things. The more a human resource manager knows about these important and monumental studies, the better they will be able to evaluate their own employees and ensure that both productivity and performance points are being consistently met at an above average level.

A focus on how an employee's race might affect their position is not related to The Hawthorne studies. The Hawthorne studies aim to look at the impact of physical influence on a company. The physical conditions a job demands will directly affect the way an employee is performing.

If they are in incredibly hot conditions all day, there's a good chance that they might not be the happiest employees. Part of the Hawthorne study also looks at the environmental factors that affect employees. Perhaps the company is located in a very cold area, so foot traffic might not be too high. Low sales could affect employee behavior, so this could be evaluated by the HRM. The Hawthorne study looks more at the things around different workers that can affect their performance rather than the mental socio-psychological factors.

Mentor

A mentor might be given to a new employee in order to act as an advisor, counselor, or other method of support during the process of training or in the beginning months as they get used to a position.

The mentor would offer advice and feedback on their behavior, as well as give tips to ensure that they find success through this process. A mentor is not to be seen as an authority figure such as someone that would fire, punish, or reprimand the employee. They might suggest behavior modification or present information to a human resource manager should the employee break a serious rule or commit a crime.

Chapter 5 – Employee and Labor Relations

Even though unions might not be as popular as they used to be, knowing all about them and the legalities involved is crucial for anyone wanting to take the test. There is still a very large portion of the test that will cover different union and labor laws.

Proper working conditions need to be maintained, whether it's through the physical layout and safety of a company or through the strategies and methods they use to train and evaluate employees.

There needs to be an understanding of the organizational climate of a company as well as the ability to resolve employee complaints. There are some methods that complaints could be handled, and in a union setting something such as a grievance procedure might be used. Knowing about all of these procedures, programs, and practices is important for those managers taking the test.

Sometimes, a human resource manager might also be responsible for processing terminations. There are many legalities and regulations that come along with firing someone from their position, and this knowledge will be tested on the exam. It's important to make sure all is known about how to properly let someone go, as well as the different forms of layoffs that might arise in a different company.

A human resource manager needs to understand a culture's organizational features and whether or not this might affect working conditions. There are different theories and practices involved in analyzing a workspace and the overall productivity of that workspace. Any applicant that wants to take the test should have a solid understanding of all of this.

Not only do applicants need to know all of the programs, federal laws, rules, regulations, and acts that affect employers and protects worker's rights, but they also need to be able to apply these. There might be different scenarios presented in which an example is used to express a potential real-life situation. A human resource manager needs to have the ability to asses this different scenario and determine if they know which law applies to which protection. This is important because, in the real world, a human resource manager might have to back up a lower-level employee that is being mistreated by someone that holds a high level of power.

One of the most important aspects that a human resource manager might have to be in charge of is a company's diversity. For too long in American history, there has been a huge lack of diversity in the workforce, with many people passed over because of their race, religion, sex, or gender. As a human resource manager, you will have to be able to identify these different instances of discrimination and understand the proper way to go about resolving the issue so everything is dealt with in a fair and legal way.

Human resource managers should be neutral when it comes to different cultures, backgrounds, and sexes, at least in their working environment. They need to understand what discrimination looks like at its core and how to identify it even when other people might not be aware.

Human resource managers need to be ready and prepared for any kind of discrimination or unfair treatment, and they need to know what to do if faced with a serious issue that could affect the integrity of the business.

A human resource manager that's taking the test needs to be aware of all levels of conflict resolution. This might just involve getting someone their tips they missed out on the previous week, or it could be as big as solving a workplace injury that resulted from two employees fighting. The different levels of severity might be found in the same section, so it is important for human resource managers taking the test to be ready and prepared for any situation.

Those taking the test need to understand the differences among employees in certain workforces and how they interact among others. Different methods of study could come in handy for this section and applying old research methods can help to identify current problems.

HR managers need to be aware of how union and non-union workers are allowed to interact with each other in the workplace, and they need to be cautious of different union recruitment tactics. They also need to understand all the different types of union shops, strikes, and which are illegal, and which are not.

Labor relations might also include performance reviews, promotions, and recognition programs. Sometimes, these all need to be discussed with a manager as well.

This is one of the longest sections on the test, so before getting into more specific details of what should be known, here is a bit more to add to your checklist of things needed to be studied before the test:

- Recordkeeping and the requirements of what should be recorded

- The inclusion of diversity and different awareness programs involved in making transitions smooth among employees of different backgrounds.

- Illness, injury, and prevention when there are different accidents that occur in a workplace. The definition of these injuries as well as what can be done to resolve them is more important information that one needs to understand before going in to take the test.

- All workplace safety and security risks. This will get touched on more in the risk management section, but there are different rules for some aspects of a working environment that should be considered with labor relations as well.

- Emergency response, whether it's to a work-related injury or death, as well as disaster recovery processes and the investigations involved in work-related accidents.

- Business continuity, in terms of who is hired and who is looked pass. There can't be a mistreatment of one protected group and favoritism of another.

- The security surrounding record keeping and the data that has been collected. This can be valuable information for competitors, so it's important to protect all training and operational programs and methods, as well as the personal information of one's employees.

- Collective bargaining and its origin, as well as all terms and concepts associated with a labor union, or other workplace organization that protects a worker's rights.

- The way that performance can be evaluated, as well as how the human resources process can be analyzed as well.

There are three phases that are involved in labor relations. The first one is union organizing. This occurs when workers start to evaluate their own rights and needs, determining if there are steps they need to take in order to increase benefits and decrease inequalities.

The second step would be collective bargaining or negotiation of the agreements of labor. This might include different tactics and strategies to resolve conflict with the employer. The third phase is the administration of contracts, which involves drafting legal agreements with employers to ensure what was discussed is carried out through an agreement.

Collective Bargaining

Collective bargaining is not a phase in labor relations. Recognition, negotiation and administration are all phases in labor relations. Collective bargaining is the act of negotiation with wages or other employee conditions, specifically carried out by an organized group that was typically chosen as others to serve as representation for the thoughts and feelings of the majority.

Collective bargaining might typically be done by the union leaders, or by one representative that was elected by others to be the voice for concern. The Civil Service Reform Act of 1978 protected the rights of workers to organize collective bargaining unions, ensuring that all workers would be allowed to fight for their rights without fear of reprimand.

Unions

The most common types of workers to be in

unions are laborers. These might include machinists, auto workers, electrical workers, or other positions of general labor. This is not the limit of the type of job that can be unionized, however. These unions might have their own bargaining unit as well.

A bargaining unit is a selected group of workers that might be the voice of the rest of the workers. They work closely together in a community of shared interests in order to represent the labor union. Knowing the different types of bargaining units and unionized organizations is important, and knowing specific names and titles is helpful as well, both on the test and in a professional setting.

A union organizer that is working within a company that union wants to unionize is referred to as "salting." Salting is the process of a union laborer getting a position of employment with the intention of unionizing that job. A person who does this is referred to as a salt.

This is a legal strategy, even though in some workplace settings, the discussion of unions between members and nonmembers is illegal.

If someone is caught salting in a new position, they might be legally fired for not showing genuine interest in a job. Human resource managers should be aware of this tactic to look out for in the hiring process. While not all salters have negative intentions, they might waste training hours and costs if they lie about the time that they plan to spend in a certain position.

Sometimes, an employee might decide that they no longer wish to be represented by their union. If this is the case, they will have to undergo a decertification election. Before that can be done, there must be at least a thirty percent petition for the election, with signatures submitted 60-90 days before a contract is to end. When it comes time for a decertification election, the person that wishes to leave the union will have to receive a majority vote.

Each union creates their own terms and representative resolutions, but there are certain factors that all union officers and human resource managers should know when it comes time for a union election. Once an election occurs, there are many different things that might occur, but before it can even happen, the union workers must show interest. A need for an election must be presented, and at least thirty percent of union workers have to agree to this election for it to take place.

Grievance Procedure

In a union setting, there might be times that disputes arise in which a settlement needs to be reached. In order to resolve conflict, a grievance procedure might be used in order to keep things professional and productive.

The process starts with a written letter to an employer from the union member, in which the grievance would be outlined. This might deal with anything from monetary compensation to personal interactions. The grievance is unique and whatever the employee is experiencing. After that, a meeting will occur in which the grievance will be discussed, and afterward, there will be a settlement.

The point of a grievance procedure is to hopefully come to a resolution in order to fix a conflict that arose. Sometimes, this might mean drafting up a new contract or increasing a certain wage. There are different reasons why a grievance procedure might occur, but many of the steps will be similar once one is decided upon.

If there is no resolution that is met in order to fix a problem, then a third-party determination might come in handy. A third-party determination is when someone else might come in to help find a resolution, and they might even do some speaking or discussing on behalf of one of the members involved in a grievance procedure. Conflict resolution is the purpose of a grievance procedure in a union setting.

Types

A firm that requires employers to pay union fees if they refuse to join the union is known as an agency shop.

There are many different types of unions that one might experience either in a human resource manager or other employment position. Some unions require membership, others don't. It's important to be aware of all the different types of unions in order to ensure that all the proper rules and regulations are being followed. An agency shop is a union in which an employer could hire union or non-union workers.

Upon employment, that new worker can either join the union or not, based on whatever they would like. If they decide not to join in, they would have to pay a certain fee in order to cover the various collective bargaining.

Members are to become part of the union within a specified time period in a union shop. A union shop might also be referred to as a post-entry closed shop, either on the test or in a professional setting. It is a form of union security in which those that are hired must join a union within a specified period of time.

This enables employees to get a chance to know if they like the position before they decide to commit to that particular union. Every union would create their own specifications for the amount of time that someone has before they make their final decision of whether or not they are going to end up joining the union shop.

Strikes

There are many different strikes that a union might start, and it's important to know the differences between them. An economic strike will happen if a union and employer failed to elicit a new contract that the union wanted in the first place. A union labor practice is one that would come about because the company has asked or been caught up in some illegal behavior or activity. A wildcat strike is one that is unauthorized and usually spontaneous or unplanned. A sympathy strike is one that occurs in support of another strike that is occurring. Knowing all about the different types of strikes is important in order to understand the different rights and agreements that workers and employers have with each other.

A wildcat strike is one that is unapproved by a union. A lockout, secondary, and economic strike are all types of strikes that have been approved by a union before taking place. Before striking, there must be an agreement among the leaders of a union. This is to ensure that this is the proper action to take.

Sometimes, a strike might cause more harm than good, so it's important to make sure that doing one is going to elicit a productive change rather than just be the reaction of some heated emotions. A wildcat strike occurs when there is not any approval from the leading members of a union. A wildcat strike might also be known as an unofficial industrial action.

When a strike has been threatened, it can cause serious tension in the workplace. Most of the time, a strike is the last thing anyone wants to do. Usually, there can be steps taken before a union goes through with a strike. In the chance that it still occurs, a human resource manager needs to be prepared for what to do next. Their main concern is going to be about how service will be maintained as well as any necessary production of the company.

Will services need to be halted, or can another department take on these duties? Of course, the media might get involved, but this shouldn't be the concern of the HRM. There might be money lost and supplies wasted as well, but this would be the concern for someone other than the HRM. It takes an entire union to organize and carry out a strike, so it cannot be blamed on one person either, and if it is, that is in a violation of the very Act that stands in place to protect union workers.

Protective Laws and Acts

As an employee and as an HR manager, it's important for one to know their rights.

Title VII of the Civil Rights Act

Title VII of the Civil Rights Act prohibits employers with 15 or more workers from discriminating, whether it's in an employment, public service, transportation, public accommodations, or telecom position.

Title VII of the Civil Rights Act states:

> "It shall be an unlawful employment practice for an employer ... to discriminate against any individual with respect to his compensation, terms,

conditions, or privileges of employment, because of such individual's race, color, religion, sex, or national origin."

This protects workers from discrimination that are in positions of employment involved in public service or public transportation, and other accommodations or telecom positions. No person can be discriminated against during hiring or firing, compensation, promotion, layoff, recall, recruitment, or pay. A human resource manager needs to be very aware of everything this act protects in order to ensure employees are treated fairly.

Americans with Disabilities Act

Title IV of the Americans with Disabilities Act prohibits mandatory retirement based on an employee's age. The Americans with Disabilities Act is in place to protect anyone that might have a disability. Disabilities include hearing impairments, physical disabilities, and anything else that might give certain workers unfair disadvantages.

In order to ensure these workers don't get discriminated against, the Americans with

Disabilities Act covers everything that an employee needs to ensure they will not be discriminated against for any impairments they might experience. This also covers pregnancy, as that will be considered a short-term disability should an employee become pregnant while working for a company.

The Americans with Disabilities Act states that when listing a job description, the most important duty should be listed first in order to give applicants a clear idea of the expectations that might be required of them should they end up in that specific position.

The Labor Management Relations Act

The Labor Management Relations Act protects workers that are in a union from termination and discrimination from their employer based on the fact that they are in a union. The Labor Management Relations Act might also be referred to as the Taft-Hartley Act. It stands to protect workers involved in unions as well as the right of workers to unionize.

It lays out that if workers are not given the opportunity to actively protect their individual and professional rights, then they could cause strikes that might upset the balance of production and commerce.

It also goes on to ensure that employees in a union versus those that are not cannot be discriminated against because of their union status. It is important for human resource managers to be aware of the importance of this act in order to protect union workers rights and be able to easily identify if something wrong is being done.

The Taft-Hartley Act amended the NLRA and addressed unfair labor union practices. The Taft-Hartley Act might also be referred to as the Labor Management Relations Act. This was put in place in order to restrict certain powers that unions have.

It also restricts certain activities and makes it so that laborers have to communicate with their employers about the different activities they plan to involve themselves in. This also requires union leaders to take on a non-communist oath, as well as make closed shops illegal. While unions have many legal rights, employers of different unions do as well, and they need to ensure that unions don't have too much strength to where they can take advantage of their power in numbers.

A human resource manager should know the differences, power balances, and what's allowed to occur between unions and employers as well as what goes on within unions that might be illegal as well.

Closed shops were made illegal with the Taft-Hartley Act in order to ensure that employers retained a certain amount of power and the activities of unions were limited. In response to the outlaw of closed shops, union shops became popular, which involve employees to have to join a union within a certain amount of time.

This gives employers the chance to pick from a wider pool while also ensuring that union workers have a say over who gets hired as well. Using a union shop versus a closed shop gives a more diverse pool for who might be accepted into the interview process.

Chapter 6 – Risk Management

Safety is one of the most important aspects for a human resource manager to understand. Though there are other departments in place that will help ensure safety standards are being met, it's still up to the human resource manager to oversee all of these aspects in order to make sure they properly carry out different legal procedures.

Risk management used to be referred to as "occupational health, safety, and security." It's essentially the same thing, but now a bit more seems to be covered in the area of "risk." This might include more than just the physical harm of the company.

Risk management is also related to personnel risk. In order to properly pass the test, takers need to be aware of all the forms of personnel risk and how they might be best avoided. Personnel risk might refer to fraud that occurs within a business. They might analyze methods in which employee behavior is tracked, especially when working with finances and voids. They would look to this in order to ensure that there aren't any employees that are taking monetary advantage of a company.

Risk management also includes making sure that all errors are avoided. Sometimes, a simple mistake could really throw an entire business off-track. Someone dealing with risk management would do their absolute best to make sure that there are no errors. They might implement different error-prevention programs and oversee different departments that are in place to make error checks. The methods for doing this should be well known and understood in order to be prepared to go into the test on exam day.

A huge part of risk management is also physical assets. This might include the insurance policies in place to protect different aspects of an office or the production and supply risks that could halt a business's income. Protecting the physical assets of a business environment is crucial in order to maintain that all the employees of a company aren't out of a job should something happen.

Disaster prevention methods should be closely studied by those that are going to take the exam. Though some things might not even occur in someone's professional career, they still need to be prepared with this information in order to properly handle whatever might be thrown at them.

HR managers are responsible for ensuring the protection of different technological aspects, which might include installing virus protection programs on the computers of employees. By making sure there is security over all electronic devices, a human resource manager is making sure that all of the company's information is protected, as well as the privacy of the employees. The HR manager might not put these protection agencies in place themselves, but would oversee that they were happening, whether it was through an IT or security department. The methods of taking proper electronic security steps should be well known to anyone going into the test.

Work relationships are also very important in understanding when it comes to risk management. Sometimes, there might be different kinds of lawsuits that a human resource manager would have to deal with.

They might have to be the mediator between two employers, or worse, their boss and a lower-level employee. Being aware of all the legal acts that protect workers rights will only help make this process go smoother should a human resource manager ever have to experience this.

Once risk has been assessed, it is also important to understand how to handle it should it happen. This might include filling out the proper forms and checking in with the right department to make sure that everything is being taken care of and smoothed over.

Risk management includes developing systems and implementing programs in order to ensure integrity and safety are maintained and managed among different employees and relationships throughout a company.

When the physical well-being of any person is protected, it is known as safety.

Having little personal control in a job is one of the biggest stress causers in a workplace environment. In order to properly assess what might cause an employee's behavior, it is important to look at everything that might illicit stress or figure out any cause of emotion that could affect their work habits.

One of the biggest causes of stress in a workplace is when an employee feels as though they don't have much personal control. This can cause them to feel as though they are falling behind, and they might not perform as well if they don't have the confidence it takes to know that they can take charge and be confident.

Standards that include general requirements for which machinery is protected in order to ensure it doesn't cause any hazard to employees or the operator is known as machine guarding. The act of guarding a machine, or a training program required by anyone that will come in contact with a hazardous machine within their first thirty days of employment, would have different terms.

Machine guarding involves different rules as well as various physical materials that protect employees from dangerous machines. These standards weren't always in place, but by requiring that certain machines have certain protecting guards, the safety of the employees that are around that machine isn't in jeopardy.

Any machine that might have flying chips,

rotating parts, or sparks might require machine guarding. This will usually be very brightly colored in order remind those around that dangerous parts exist underneath.

Falls are the leading cause of death in the workplace. The other three are: electrocution, getting struck by an object and getting caught in-between objects.

The leading place of death of individuals in the workplace are those involved in the construction industry. The Fatal Four is a term coined by OSHA that describes the top four cause of deaths in the construction industry. The first is fatal falling which accounts for over 1-3rd of construction deaths. The following three in the fatal four are electrocution, getting struck by an object, and getting caught in between objects.

Occupational Safety and Health Act

At one point in history, it was cheaper to replace dead or injured workers rather than put safety regulations in place that protected these workers. In order to maintain morality, The Occupational Safety and Health Act passed in

1970 to ensure that companies were doing everything they could to ensure no injury or death occurred that could have been easily prevented.

It is important to remember these years in order to relate them to just how recently workers went without some of these basic rights and protections. It is also important for human resource managers to understand the history of workplace safety in order to prevent it from happening again. While some specific years can be challenging to remember, these precise bits of information are needed to make sure that the test is properly passed.

According to the United States Department of Labor, the Occupational Safety and Health Act exists, "To assure safe and healthful working conditions for working men and women; by authorizing enforcement of the standards developed under the Act; by assisting and encouraging the States in their efforts to assure safe and healthful working conditions; by providing for research, information, education, and training in the field of occupational safety and health; and for other purposes."

1970 is when The Occupational Safety and

Health Act passed. The Occupational Safety and Health Administration sets standards for employees in terms of safety and health. They are the administration that is in charge of ensuring employees are taken care of, and if an injury does occur, it is handled properly. There are many different interactions a human resource manager might have with someone from OSHA, so the more aware they are of what is going on within the operations of OSHA, the better they will be able to resolve an issue should one arise.

The dealings with OSHA, such as what forms or procedures need to be dealt with, is important in order to ensure the proper recordings are done. For example, OSHA uses something known as a form 200 to record illnesses, accidents, and injuries. That term alone might be something often discussed within a company and with specific human resource managers and their employees.

Safety Management

Organizational, engineering, and individual are

the three approaches to effective safety management. Human resources is not considered one of them and are instead representative of the collective of the three. There are many different procedures a company can choose to use within their safety department and to protect workers. There are some key approaches that should be known by all human resource managers for how different safety management will be effectively used.

One is an organizational approach. What is occurring within an organization that provides safety, and what organizational factors need to be improved upon in order to ensure safety measurements are being reached. Another approach is engineering. Are certain mechanics safe, and are there processes to using machines that are in place to make sure all workers are protected? Another approach is individual. Are the employees safe on an individual level, and can those around an employee feel safe among their fellow workers?

Safety hierarchy refers to the order that actions should be taken in order to eliminate work safety problems. A safety hierarchy can be in reference to the processes of risk control. There are a certain number of actions that need to be taken in order to make sure work safety problems are eliminated.

The first step is to identify anything that might be hazardous or dangerous. A human resource manager has to look around a workplace and the environment that workers will be subjected to and identify each and every hazard that might cause an employee potential harm. The second would be risk identification.

Is there a risk or chance that something might happen? After that, risk assessment and risk control follow to ensure all of these problems are properly dealt with, or that there is at least a plan in place to help if something does happen to go wrong. The final two steps of the hierarchy involve documenting and monitoring the process and continuing the process of keeping everything safe and hazard-free.

Ergonomics

Ergonomics is a work environment design that is the most proper for addressing physical demands that are experienced by people within a business. Ergonomics is the study of how people work efficiently within the environment they are employed. A human resource manager will have extensive knowledge of ergonomics and the practices and studies that come along with the various theories involved with how an employee interacts with their environment.

Ergonomics aims to refine products, tools, and services that help make people's jobs much easier. Ergonomics might involve designing a more efficient desk or computer chair, or it might be more extensive such as developing the method in which a company does the hiring.

MSDS

When a hazardous chemical is processed, stored, or used, an MSDS would be required. An MSDS is a material safety data sheet. These forms are required when there is any handling of a hazardous chemical. Whether this chemical is processed, stored, or used, an MSDS is required in order to make sure that the activity is properly monitored.

They might be placed directly in the workplace, or right where certain hazardous materials are kept and stored. They are reminders to those around that there is hazardous material nearby and certain safety precautions need to be used in order to make sure that no harm can come to the employees involved with it. This also protects employers, as it gives employees the responsibility of properly dealing with these chemicals and materials.

Polygraph Instances

When hiring a guard or member of a security firm that would be responsible for, or have access to, a controlled substance is an instance in which a polygraph test might be administered. Employers are not allowed to give polygraph tests whenever they want, or when an employee calls off sick without a doctor's note. If more than $500 worth of company property goes missing, a police investigation might follow, in which, in rare circumstances, a polygraph test would be administered.

Employers are not allowed to give polygraph tests whenever they want, or when an employee calls off sick without a doctor's note. If more than $500 worth of company property goes missing, a police investigation might follow, in which, in rare circumstances, a polygraph test would be administered.

Most of the time, however, polygraphs are only given when it is important to protect some aspect of security in a job. Whether they are working with classified information or substances that can cause destruction and harm, a polygraph test will likely be administered, but mostly, at the discretion of the HRM or others higher up in the position. Sometimes, if the employee refuses to take a polygraph test, they might not be able to get hired for that position.

Injuries

The overall definition of safety is the condition of protection. When one person can be certain that everything is in place necessary to ensure that they can't get hurt, they will perform much better. It is a natural human instinct to want to feel safe. It is in our biology, so of course, when workers feel like they are safe and protected, they will be able to perform much better than if they were in any other situation.

Accident Investigation

Talking to the person that was injured as well as a witness is very important if an employer wants to conduct an accident investigation and properly fill out the reports. Some companies might exist without ever having to worry about having an accident or causing one of their employee's harm.

Unfortunately, there are plenty of work environments that are prone to accidents, but there are steps to be taken to prevent and resolve workplace accidents. One of the first steps of starting an accident investigation is to isolate the accident scene. The first step is important in making sure that no one else can end up getting hurt in the same way. This is also important to make sure that the scene can't be altered in a situation that might destroy evidence.

The injured worker should be removed immediately, of course, in order to receive proper treatment. The next step is to record any evidence to ensure that it was a complete accident and not something intentional, or something caused by negligence. Recording is also vital in this. After the scene has been assessed, it is time to identify witnesses and speak to the employee that was injured, as long as they are healthy enough and in a state that they can recall what happened.

If an injury or death has occurred, this is considered a recordable case. Some injuries or accidents don't always need to be recorded if they are not very serious. OSHA has certain standards that lay out whether or not an injury is recordable or needs to be recorded.

If it is an injury that cannot be treated with first aid, such as a minor cut, bump, or burn, then it must be recorded. Anytime an employee has to spend days away from work because of the accident or seek professional medical treatment, they need to record their injury.

If there is a loss of consciousness, or even worse, death, this is certainly something that needs to be recorded. If it is an injury that is not work-related, it does not need to be recorded by OSHA.

Drug Use

Disability injuries, injury and illness related deaths, and minor injuries are all defined by the Occupational Safety and Health Act.

Employers can choose who they want to drug test. If drug tests are chosen, they can be conducted in whichever way the employee prefers, including taking blood, urine, or hair samples. Employers don't have to drug test everyone they hire, though they do have to stay consistent with the group they choose to test.

Employers have the right to decide if they want to drug test their candidates or not, but if they choose to do so, they have to ensure that they are being fair with those they pick to test. Only choosing to test a certain candidate is not fair and can be an act of discrimination.

However, only choosing to test employees with more important duties than those with other positions is a common practice. For instance, at a hotel, those that are in high managerial positions might have to be drug tested, but maids or concierge don't have as many responsibilities, so employers might save money by choosing to not test this specific category of workers. In order to ensure there is no discrimination taking place, employers have to make sure they're maintaining consistency with who is being tested.

The Drug-Free Workplace Act

The Drug-Free Workplace Act is in place to inform employees of what might be a violation, spreading awareness, and training supervisors. It does not consider tobacco and alcohol as controlled substances, and it only applies to those employers that have contracts or grants with the government.

One thing a human resource manager might run into often is drug use within the workplace. Some companies might fall under the Drug-Free Workplace Act of 1988, in which a specific grant is received by the company to ensure that they're creating a drug-free work zone. This might involve issuing drug tests and doing extensive background checks on employees to ensure that no drug abuse is taking place.

Those companies that are given grants because of The Drug-Free Workplace Act must inform employees of certain dangers or violations that should occur if drug use is detected. Not all Human resource managers will work for a company that falls under The Drug-Free Workplace Act, but it is still important to be aware of this Act in order to pass the test.

Chapter 7 – Learning and Development

Learning and development is a newer section on the test, so in various study guides and practice quizzes, you might not see this section depending on the year in which the information was written. The basic ideas of this section correlate with the ideas of training and development as well.

Learning and development is all about the contribution to an organizations learning activities. This might include different programs of education to continually teach employees the information they need, or a program that offers assistance in attaining certain degrees or certifications.

This also goes over development, which would include implementation and evaluation of various programs, with an internal consultation and data provider that would help assess the necessity of the programs that have been put in place.

An important part of this section is understanding the types of consultation and evaluation that can be given to different managers as well as employees that will help them grow professionally, and possibly even personally depending on the company and the morals that are involved. Different developmental activities will also be assessed with employers to determine what can change about a business in order for it to be more productive.

As innovations continue to make life easier for some, they also provide more information to others that can be hard to process. This section is more relevant now as human resource managers have to go over different data analytic methods and look at how they might apply to the learning and development of their company.

A human resource manager will be responsible for contributing succession plans, which would involve the preparation of certain employees for different positions that they are not in just yet. The succession plan would include everything that would be involved in training them and making sure they are prepared to take on their new duties and responsibilities.

Assessing data is important in order to see where costs can be cut, where areas need attention, and what methods of training or development might not have been working thus far. As more tools emerge that can help with assessing data, there's more information that these human resource managers need to learn in order to provide their companies with the most effective knowledge.

Learning and development are both important, but there are also laws and regulations that are in place to protect certain aspects of these as well. Just like all the other sections that will be on the test, it is important to remember the laws put in place to cover or regulate areas of learning and development. This might include the protection of employees and their privacy rights when it comes to collecting data. Human resource managers need to make sure that only fair and legally received information is being used to assess employees and develop their skills further.

Human resource managers also need the tools to develop their own theories about a certain workplace. By taking the theories or studies of other managers, they can apply specific parts to their own company to ensure they are getting proper feedback and the information they need to make correct decisions about what developmental tools need to be implemented within their business.

Some other important aspects of learning and development that human resource managers need to study include:

- Delivery of training programs and facilitation techniques

- Adult learning processes as well as instructional design principles

- The techniques involved to assess different training programs and their efficiency

- Methods of motivation and problem-solving techniques that will aid in organizational development.

- Coaching, mentoring, retention, analysis, task, creativity, and innovative programs and practices that will aid to employee interpersonal growth

This section is all about focusing on individual employees and encouraging their development. It is crucial for human resource managers to look at their employees as people with a lot of knowledge and skill to contribute and not just someone there to perform a task. These innovative thinking processes are results of various studies that should be memorized so they can be applied to situational examples on the exam.

Much like a business lifecycle, a human resource development lifecycle has similar stages. They begin with an introduction, where a human resource manager is aware of their responsibilities, then introducing others to these methods as well.

The second stage is growth, when different aspects of HRM are being smoothed over. The next stage is maturity, when peak management is reached, and instead of dying off like a business cycle, there is a level of management to be maintained with certain standards in place that are concrete and secure.

Determination of availability can be found through the demographic information provided by affirmative action. Affirmative action is a policy that aims to protect certain groups that commonly experience discrimination by ensuring that fair opportunity is given to minorities that might otherwise be overlooked, intentionally or unintentionally.

Sometimes, there might not be as high of a demographic of protected groups in one area as there is another, so there can't be standards set for the number of employees from protected groups that should be hired. Instead, a determination of availability should be explored in order to figure out what percentage of a protected group should be represented within a specific organization.

Chapter 8 – Talent Planning and Acquisition

Talent planning and acquisition is a focus on how different talent is sought out for a position, and what needs to be done to acquire their employment. This involves looking for external sources of employees, or perhaps tracking those with specific skills that might be working in other departments.

What's most important in the acquisition process is following standard laws and regulations that protect current employees as well as those that might end up getting hired. The organizational policies that put legal and ethical requirements in place are important in each chapter, but talent planning and acquisition will especially focus on hiring laws. Some of these important laws include:

- Nepotism

- FLSA

- Independent contractors

- Title VII

- Disparate impact

These ideas might be covered in other sections, but they most apply here to talent seeking. Social media might play a role in this part as well. It won't be a huge part of the exam, but it's important to look into how social media is affecting different acquisition processes of different talent managers. There are still legal standards around using social media in a professional setting, so the test taker should be well-versed in this area as well.

Planning, in all parts of the hiring process, should be very well understood in order to properly identify which steps are right and which other ones might be completely wrong. All parts of a talent acquisition lifecycle should be understood, including the interview process, what happens when an offer is extended, background checks, drug screening, reference checks, and the negotiation process when it comes to terms of employment.

Not only is it important for human resource managers to know where and how to seek out different levels of talent, but they also need to have the abilities to assess talent overall. Are they looking in the right area? Is there a conclusion to be made about the type of applicants? This process of analysis can help better regulate the talent search.

There are likely going to be many questions on types of interviews and the interview process as well. It is important for those taking the exam to be aware of anything they might get asked in relation to interviewing and the legality of what can and cannot be asked. There are many things to include in a job description to keep the company protected from any discrimination, and in each step of acquisition after that, it seems like things only become more regulated.

Acquisition

Checking all references is important when developing hiring plans. Checking references is a way that human resource managers can be sure they are hiring the right employee. There are certain guidelines that need to be considered when checking references, however.

Some companies have rules and regulations that state their employees aren't allowed to give any past information on a particular worker other than their last name and the dates in which they were employed. This protects workers that are no longer in a company from receiving biased feedback that could be false or misinform future potential managers.

Recruiting

Promotion would not be considered external recruiting. External recruiting is any involvement in assessing outside candidates for a certain position rather than looking at the existing staff. This might be done by visiting schools that have future candidates that are about to graduate. Some companies find that hiring those with less experience will require a lower salary.

Using media sources to gauge what is available might also be a form of external recruiting. An employment agency might also be used for external recruiting in order to seek out more qualified candidates that have been carefully selected by different professionals.

Types of Contracts

In some cases, temporary work might need to be hired either to replace an employee that is going to leave, or to make up for the need of a higher workforce, perhaps in busy seasons. In order to protect the company and these temporary workers, a human resource manager might use a third-party contract in order to lay out the terms of the specific agreement between the trust and the company.

The third-party contract would include how much time is expected to be worked and the compensation that will be given for that short period of employment. These contracts might include different terms from what regular consistent employees are receiving as well.

Maintenance

HR managers should locate imbalances among their workforce, so they can remedy the underrepresentation of protected groups with affirmative action.

A citizen of one country that works in a second but is also employed by an organization that is headquartered in a third country is a third country national. It can be hard for those traveling with various visas to keep up with all the rules and regulations, but human resource managers need to be very aware of them all in order to protect the rights of their workers as well as the company from any illegal hiring.

For instance, a human resource manager should be aware of the definition of a third country national, a person that might be applying for a visa in a country that isn't their origin country, but only doing so to go to a different country in order to work. These definitions and restrictions can be confusing for some to remember, so it's important to not just memorize the specifications but also be aware of why they're there in the first place.

Turnover rates can be calculated by taking the number of terminations, times 100, and dividing it by the average number of employees.

The Family and Medical Leave Act

Up to 12 weeks of unpaid leave can be taken during a 12-month period according to The Family and Medical Leave Act, though there are standards that make the time differ depending on the situation.

The Family and Medical Leave Act might be often referred to as or written like FMLA. FMLA protects a worker's rights to take family and medical leave if they need to. They are given 12 weeks within a 12-month period. This might include taking time off for the birth of a child, as well as leave to care for the child, as well as if a child is adopted.

If an employee has a spouse, child, or other close family member with a serious health condition, they might be eligible to take FMLA leave in order to care for them. If the employee themselves has a serious health condition that keeps them from properly performing their job, they would also apply for FLMA. Twenty-six workweeks can also be taken during a 12-month period in order to care for a servicemember that has a serious illness or injury and requires the care of their family member or spouse.

MBO

Measurable goals make up a good MBO. MBO stands for management by objectives, the acronym switched around for obvious reasons. This is a six-step process that is used to integrate managerial activities to improve employee efficiency, as well as achieve corporate goals.

The first step of an MBO is to define organizational goals. This starts with creating goals that are measurable and not ones that are too high to obtain. After that, individual employee objectives should be defined in order to determine what is needed on both a corporate and an individual level. There should be a continual monitoring of progress, with a performance evaluation and feedback to follow. The last step would be a performance appraisal, and the then MBO can start over again.

Conclusion

It is up to the test taker to make sure that they will have all the knowledge necessary to pass the test. You saw in the beginning of each chapter what information is needed to know in order to make sure that preparation has been met. There are plenty of people that don't pass the test, and there is no shame in that. In order to prevent this from happening, spend some time looking at your areas of weakness. If there's a consistent theme among the ideas or questions that you don't understand, try to analyze that to figure out what you need to do to become better prepared.

Perhaps you struggle with different union laws, or maybe remembering dates is challenging. Find a method of studying that works, including flashcards or thinking of a game you can take with classmates or coworkers who are also taking the test. Do whatever you have to in order to make sure that you're understanding the information and not just memorizing it.

Make sure that you find an appropriate place to study. This might mean going to a coffee shop, library, or other place that you can find peace and quiet. Reading in your bed might be fine for certain fiction novels but sometimes studying requires more attention and focus that you won't achieve while snuggled under the covers. Give yourself plenty of time to study before the test and don't try to rush yourself. Even if you think you are prepared to take the test, you might still be lacking information in a section that could give you a low score.

Remember when studying to not completely ignore your strengths or putting emphasis on the knowledge that you're good at. Sometimes, people tend to go over the things they don't understand until they know it better than anything. They might end up neglecting parts they thought they had a decent understanding of, but that might come back to bite them on actual test day. All information needs to be known and understood at the same level.

Do not force yourself to study too much. You might feel the need to study for long hours until the information is understood, but for some people, taking in all this information can be a long process. Though the sooner the better when it comes to certification, it's better to take your time and ensure you know everything needed to pass rather than to try and cram it all in quickly just to get a passing grade. By consuming too much information too quickly, it can all be forgotten just as fast. The best way to actually get to know and understand the information needed is to take it at your own pace, one that includes learning and processing the information.

This is about your future job and status of employment. Though some information can seem tedious or non-applicable, it is all still important knowledge that can help someone not only pass the test but also improve their overall work performance.

Passing the Test

The goal is passing the test. That's why anyone would come to read a study guide. There are some key elements it takes to actually pass a test besides just having an understanding of the information.

A big thing that many people forget to do is to relax. Though the test is timed, rushing yourself will only cause panic. If you don't understand a question, skip it and go back to it later. Some people don't like doing this, but there's a chance that you'll remember the more you get into the test or even a slight chance that the answer exists within another question! Spending 10 minutes just to maybe get one question right is not going to help you pass the test. Instead, spend those ten minutes on questions you know, even if that means completely missing the mark on the one you were originally struggling with. Getting one question wrong is better than not even answering ten different questions.

Preparing for the Test

When the day of the test arrives, it's important to be prepared, relaxed, and focused for the test. Get there as early as possible and make sure to eat breakfast, drink coffee, or do whatever else you might in a normal daily routine. Having a nice meal will help you stay focused during the test without having to worry if your stomach is going to grumble. Trying chewing gum as well, as this can help keep focus.

While practicing this test multiple times can help, it's important that the concepts and ideas are understood rather than just memorized. These are not exact questions of what's going to be on the test, only examples of the information that might be presented. You can also take as many different practice tests as you want but know that you aren't likely going to be able to find any others that contain the current test questions verbatim. Instead, you have to focus on the main concepts that created the questions and figure out how these may be applicable in different scenarios.

It's important to ensure that the study guide has been studied as well and is paired with the practice test in book one. When both are studied, as well as other important information, the test-taker has a much better chance of receiving their certification.

What to Bring

Make sure on exam day that you arrive at least fifteen minutes before your scheduled time. This way, in case something does happen, you'll have already planned to be there a few minutes early so your time won't be as late had you expected to get there right on time. If you arrive too late, you risk losing your chance to take the test without getting a refund on any fees paid.

Bring your ID; the type doesn't matter as long as it's not expired, and it's government issued. This might include your passport or driver's license. If you do not bring this with you, you will not be able to receive your test or certification, no matter how knowledgeable and prepared for the information you might be. It's important to not forget small things like this in order to ensure that nothing gets in the way of you getting your certificate!

Good luck!

Lightning Source UK Ltd.
Milton Keynes UK
UKHW011124070920
369491UK00003B/608